W9-BLP-625

+
Sm55r

# THE RAILROAD BOOK

## STORY AND PICTURES BY E. BOYD SMITH

### INTRODUCTION BY ETHEL L. HEINS

HOUGHTON MIFFLIN COMPANY
BOSTON 1983

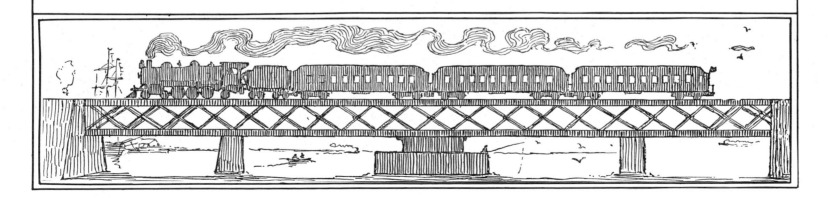

Printed in the United States of America

H   10 9 8 7 6 5 4 3 2 1

*Library of Congress Cataloging in Publication Data*

Smith, E. Boyd (Elmer Boyd), 1860–1943.
  The railroad book.

  Summary: Bob and Betty learn about trains when the
railroad opens up a line behind their garden fence.
  [1. Railroads—Trains—Fiction]   I. Title.
PZ7.S6465Rai  1983        [Fic]        83-8505
ISBN 0-395-34832-3

# INTRODUCTION

For a long time, until the late 1920s, fine picture books for children in this country consisted largely of imports from abroad. The famous nineteenth-century English triumvirate of Walter Crane, Randolph Caldecott, and Kate Greenaway continued to dominate the field. But the works of turn-of-the-century illustrators from England and the Continent — like Beatrix Potter, Leslie Brooke, and Maurice Boutet de Monvel — moved into prominence and were proudly displayed in the newly organized children's rooms of our great metropolitan libraries.

Yet a careful look at the roots of American picture books reveals a remarkable figure, both prolific and popular, whose beautiful picture books were read, pored over, and loved by countless children for several decades. Elmer Boyd Smith was born in 1860 in New Brunswick, Canada, and grew up in Boston; after a long period spent studying and working in France, he finally settled in Connecticut. By the time he died, in 1943, he had illustrated more than seventy books, not only for children but for adults as well — everything from picture books to such classics as *Ivanhoe, The Last of the Mohicans,* and Benjamin Franklin's *Autobiography.*

It is not surprising that E. Boyd Smith's early picture books were influenced by contemporaneous European art. One finds, for example, the genial humor of Leslie Brooke in *The Story of Noah's Ark* (1905); and *The Story of Pocahontas and Captain John Smith* (1906) was no less a triumph because it was patently inspired by the splendor of Boutet de Monvel's *Joan of Arc.* But in response to a clear call for good picture books from the influential Clara Hunt, director of children's work at the Brooklyn Public Library, E. Boyd Smith's *The Farm Book* was published in 1910; and even though the handsome volume owed an obvious debt to the *plein-air* painting of the Swedish Carl Larsson, it was equally obvious that Smith's work was becoming vigorously American. The forthright Miss Hunt, pleased at last, declared that the book came "nearer to satisfying our ideals of what a picture book should be than anything heretofore done by an American artist."

*The Farm Book,* projected through the experiences of the children Bob and Betty, was followed two years later by *The Seashore Book;* and in 1913 *The Railroad Book* was published. Houghton Mifflin auspiciously brought *The Farm Book* back into print in 1982; now a further source of satisfaction is the return of *The Railroad Book.*

One might claim that the appeal of the book would be purely nostalgic; but nostalgia is an adult wistfulness — not a childlike emotion — a romantic yearning for things vanished and unrecoverable. On the contrary, the book's attraction lies in its aesthetic quality and in its representation of something vibrantly American. The railroads, after all, shaped, unified, and built our country, ultimately enriching our vocabulary and our folklore; moreover, despite their faded grandeur, they refuse to disappear. And many present day space-age children who have never ridden on a train are nevertheless fascinated by the magic and mystique of railroading.

In this book, E. Boyd Smith captured with words and pictures the ingenuous awe and enthusiasm in a youthful response to railroads. A newly laid track spur brought trains and trainmen close to the home of Bob and Betty. What excitement! Soon they learned to recognize various engines by their characteristic whistles and to distinguish passenger and freight trains by their sounds. The children felt boundless admiration for the train crews and made friends with engineers, firemen, and brakemen; they were even taken to see the "great monsters, iron horses, puffing and snorting" in the round house. Betty and Bob especially loved the bustling little station, with its glorious confusion of incoming freight, and the brother and sister traveled to the city to the huge new central station, "as imposing as a cathedral." Finally, with their parents they made the long journey by rail from the Atlantic to the Pacific, crossing mountains, rivers, and prairies in day coaches, sleepers, and dining cars — an almost unbelievable adventure for two children.

Totally respectful of young readers, E. Boyd Smith seventy years ago gave them an abundance of information in an uncondescending, nondidactic text written with a kind of dignified informality. And the clarity and freshness of the verbal expression infuses all of the illustrations. Forms and shapes are defined by crisp, careful drawing; and the wealth of details enlivening the pictures is always precise and orderly — as in nineteenth-century French realistic painting. The artist's extraordinary sense of both color and composition lends a serene — but never static — atmosphere, while the skillful, judicious use of perspective quietly heightens the dramatic effects. E. Boyd Smith's *The Railroad Book* celebrates a lively aspect of America's past with a gracious combination of idealism and realism.

Ethel L. Heins
Auburndale, Massachusetts

# ON THE FENCE

This year the railroad built a new spur of track which ran close behind the fence of Bob and Betty's garden, and the children were keenly interested in the work as it advanced day by day. Gangs of swarthy laborers vigorously wielded shovel and pick, cutting through knolls and levelling the grade. Then the wooden "sleepers" were laid and the steel tracks spiked down upon them. The busy hand-car, going back and forth, excited Bob and Betty's admiration. Bob tried hard to make his express wagon into one, but somehow it wouldn't work. Of course, they asked many questions, and were told all about the first railroad, away off in England, long ago, and how from that start railroads sprang up everywhere, and now ran to pretty nearly all the places in their geographies. How the trains brought to the people of the cities food: wheat and meat from the great plains of the West, so far away; till the subject of railroads became to Bob and Betty as interesting as a real fairy story.

When the first train ran over the new track, great was the children's enthusiasm. They felt as though it was their own train. They made themselves a good lookout on the back fence and climbed up on boxes they had arranged in steps. And whenever the *toot! toot!* of the engine was heard afar off, they dropped everything and ran to their lookout. They got to know the engines by their whistles, and knew the freight train by its sound. They could always tell you whether it was a passenger or freight train coming. Their admiration for the brakeman was whole-hearted as they watched him wave his arms as a signal to go ahead, back, etc., and occasionally flag another train to stop, to give some instruction. He was the hero of the car-tops.

And now railroad became the popular game. Bob was the engine and puffed and stamped, with *choo! choo!* getting up steam, while Betty in the express wagon was passenger and train. They didn't forget the flags, and by this time knew just what each was used for. They could tell you that the engine with white flags on top was an extra, a special. And, of course, green flags were always flying on the rear of trains. The red flag, as everybody knew, meant stop.

## GETTING ACQUAINTED

This new interest, the railroad, outdid the farm and seashore in excitement. The thundering rush of the express train was always rather alarming, though fascinating. And the slow and deliberate freights, which often stopped on the switch, to let some other train go by, were an endless source of interest. Coal cars, cattle cars, cars loaded with everything imaginable, from trees to wagons and carriages, and cars from many different railroads — all mixed in the same train.

But the caboose was the car the children fell in love with. Here the trainmen lived, had their stove, and beds, and the lookout on top where they could oversee the whole train.

Daring brakemen freely walked along the tops of the cars, their blouses blowing in the wind.

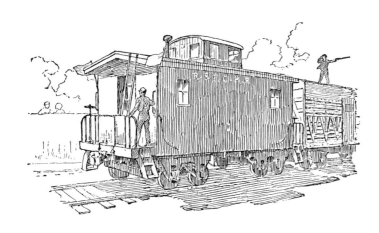

Gradually the children were tempted to go out through their back gate, it was so handy, though old Uncle Eben, the gardener, was nervous about it. They got acquainted with the train crews, and watched the engineer oil his great shiny monster of an engine, with that fascinating long-snouted oil-can. The hissing clouds of steam were rather disconcerting at times, but Bob and Betty soon learned to know where they came from, and could avoid those danger spots.

They were curious to know what was in those two big domes on top of the boiler. The engineer explained that they held sand, which was led by pipes down in front of the big driving-wheels, to be used when needed on the slippery rails. Finding them so interested, he showed them all around the engine and explained the different parts. But I am not sure that Bob and Betty understood it all. Bob, at any rate, while waiting for the next train, now had to oil his engine as he had seen the engineer do. Of course, it was the same express wagon, and the watering-can had to take the place of the engineer's oil-can. Still, that was the best he could do, and it gave the idea.

# THE RIDE IN THE CAB

One day they had a real treat, one that few children ever know. The engineer invited them for a short ride in the cab, just down to the water tank. It seemed too much like a dream to be true. They climbed up the high steps, or rather they were helped up, for the cab floor was as high as the top of a man's head from the ground. It was all rather grimy, coal dust was thick, and I don't believe their mother was pleased when she saw their clothes after this ride. But then they only did it once. In the cab everything seemed to the children a general confusion of boiler, pipes, valves, gauges, and brakes. The engineer, with his hand on the throttle, let in the steam and started up. The fireman shoveled coal into the yawning furnace door, and slowly they moved ahead. The cab had little room for passengers, but Bob and Betty, perched on the fireman's seat, were fairly comfortable, though they had to hold on, for the cab shook and rocked in a startling manner. Out through the windows they had a splendid

view of the tracks stretching away off ahead; forever, it seemed to them. Down by the side of the track was the watering-tank, set up on high stilts. Here the engines were given a drink, when thirsty. They ran up beside it, stopped, the fireman swung the big water-pipe over the tender, and turned on the water. He splashed the coal first to wash away the dust, which often gets in the engineer's eyes, and then filled their own tank, which is in the tender, under the coal: from here it is led to the boiler as needed.

The engineer, after lifting Betty and Bob down, showed them just how this water supply worked. He pointed out as well the scoop under the tender, for sometimes the train scoops up its water supply while running, as it passes over a trough between the tracks.

It was all very interesting to the children, and they made up their minds to keep a sharp lookout for a watering-trough, a "track tank," as the railroad men call it.

# THE ROUND HOUSE

Bob and Betty, now more and more interested in railroads, besieged Uncle Eben with questions which he found hard to answer, and he offered to take them to the railroad yard where they could see more than he could tell them about. They got permission from their parents, and he took them on the trolley to the "round house." This was the place where the engines were brought together, to be cleaned and looked over, and got ready for taking out their trains. It was a most impressive sight, so many of these great monsters, iron horses, puffing and snorting, the air above them filled with steam and smoke. They looked like huge animals, living creatures. Busy men climbed over them and wiped off grime and coal dust, putting them into a bright and shining shape again, after their last trips. Others looked them over thoroughly to see that nothing was broken or out of order.

Uncle Eben met a friend here who explained to them all about the different engines. He pointed out the "Moguls," and the "Compounds," the "Superheateds," the "Atlantics," and the "Pacifics," the famous "So and So flyer," the great freight engines, the "Hogs," he called them, the "Battle Ships," and so on, for the railroad men have different names for the types of engines. The children already knew the "Grasshopper."

To Bob and Betty these railroad people seemed like "land sailors," a special people who had a world of their own, different and distinct from anything else. They lived in coal dust and talked a language not understood by others, and of things which the rest of the world didn't seem to know anything about. They were quite fascinating.

From time to time an engine would be called for, its train was ready, it would be shunted onto the "turn table," whirled around to its track, and away it would go. And so through the afternoon they went, one by one, off to their duty, while others, weary from their work, came in to rest and be groomed. The busy "switch" engine, different again from the others, plied back and forth, putting trains together, the same trains which Bob and Betty often saw flashing through the night on their way to some far-away town.

# THE WRECKING CAR

There had been a great rain storm, a tremendous cloud burst, and Bob and Betty heard the neighbors talking about a "washout" on the railroad. They easily induced Uncle Eben, now as interested as themselves, to take them to see the train wreck, which happened to be not too far away. Here they saw that the track had been washed away and had allowed the train to slide into the river. Fortunately nobody had been much hurt, so the accident was interesting without being tragic.

The "wrecking" train had been sent for at once, and came pulling up just about the time Bob and Betty arrived. The wrecker soon got his car in position to work. It was specially made for this purpose, and had "outriggers" which were slid out and firmly wedged up to give it a good wide base. Then the great crane was swung on the revolving body of the car, tackle was attached, strong wire cables were carried out to the cars lying on their sides, and slowly and carefully the powerful crane lifted them from the river, swinging them back to the track which still remained in place.

All this was not done very quickly; it took a good deal of time, and great care, but the big derrick easily handled the great, long cars. Bob and Betty admired it much as they would a mighty hero. After the work was done, they got a chance to see it well. The wrecker good-naturedly explained to them how it worked, though they couldn't understand it. But they could understand the tool car, with its rows of axes, shovels, crowbars, etc., neatly hung along the inside, each tool in its place, and each brightly painted red and green, so he could keep track of his own tools, the wrecker explained.

When the rescued cars were run off, at once the repairing of road-bed began. Trains of dump cars arrived, loaded with stone and earth. By an ingenious contrivance the sides were raised, and the cars spilled out their loads; laborers shoveled these where needed. And before the day was over the road-bed had been re-made and new tracks laid, and the trains were again running as though nothing had happened.

# AT THE FREIGHT HOUSE

There was always much of interest for the children at the new little station, just a few blocks from their own home. Whenever they got a chance they liked to go there with someone, to see the trains come rumbling in and stop with a snort, see the passengers get off, or get on, and hear the conductor shout "All aboard," and see him wave his hand to the engineer to go ahead. Then the "puff! puff!" of the engine, and the train would start off again.

The station agent handling the express packages and baggage, too, was interesting. He was always in a hurry, as the trains couldn't stop long, running up to the baggage car in front. Here stray trunks, and many express packages, were dumped out, and others taken on, while the busy agent answered questions and tried to keep track of everything at once.

One day Uncle Eben was sent down to get something which had come by freight. He took Bob and Betty, of course, for they never missed a chance.

When they got to the freight house they had to get off in a corner out of the rush, for a train had just come in and was unloading. The busy men, hurrying as usual, were carrying the freight across the tracks into the freight house, where the station agent was receiving it.

And such a variety of things. To the children it seemed as though there was a little of everything, from hens to big heavy pieces of machinery, which the men rolled in with great effort. Here the bustle was fast and furious; these busy, coal-grimed men tore back and forth, got their work done as quickly as possible, climbed aboard the train, and were off up the road for the next station.

So this was the way things came from far and near. Bob and Betty had never thought of it before. They wondered how it was done when there were no railroads.

Outside they saw their own coal dealer getting in his supply from some cars on the side track, and they began to see what a very important thing the railroad was. It could take you anywhere, and bring you anything from anywhere.

# IN THE DAY CAR

Occasionally Bob and Betty would go by train to the great city with their parents. The trip was always attractive to them; the busy day car, with its passengers getting on or off, the conductor slowly working his way through, punching holes in their nice new tickets, politely answering many questions, and explaining time-tables and connections; his knowledge seemed uncanny. The newsboy cheerfully and noisily hawked the daily papers and latest magazines, "just out." Bob thought his must be a romantic life, always going back and forth on these wonderful cars.

When the train rumbled over a bridge the view of the ships and docks below was full of life and variety. Sometimes the draw would be up and the train had to stop on the bridge while vessels were towed through by little bustling, important tugs. Then the draw was slowly swung back into place and the train

continued its journey, rushing through a black, smoky tunnel, to emerge into the station yard with its myriad tracks, and its many trains ceaselessly coming and going. Great works of construction were always going on, for the railroad life never seems to stand still, it is always changing, new tracks, new bridges, or new stations always building. Here they even saw trains being run by electricity, the latest form of power, doing away with smoke and coal dust, a sort of glorified trolley line. And trains and more trains, simply no end to trains.

In the city, down by the water front, to the children's great surprise they actually saw trains being carried across the bay in ferry boats, "car floats." Such a thing they had never heard of before. It seemed unbelievable, but there it was before them. They were told that this method of taking trains across the water was nearing its end, and now tunnels had been built deep down below the sea through which the trains ran just as safely as out on the open roads. This, of course, was more astonishing even than the ferry boats. But then the whole subject of railroads was so wonderful itself that they felt that wonders would never cease as far as it was concerned.

# THE CENTRAL STATION

When it came near time to go home Bob and Betty's mother took them through the new central station. It was a huge building, as imposing as a cathedral, with its great main hall, and large waiting-rooms. Everything was arranged for the convenience and comfort of the many passengers who steadily streamed through it, coming and going from trains. Book stands, and restaurants, etc., were right at hand.

Conveniently placed was the "information" bureau, where men capable of answering any imaginable question, patiently did so through the day; to the knowing they were really as remarkable as the rest of the building. Betty bought the tickets, with her mother's help, from the ticket agent behind his netting, another gifted man who could sell you a ticket to any place you might ask for.

Then they went down to their train, to wait on the platform for their father, who

was to go home with them after his day's work. This was not an ideal place to wait, as bustling crowds hurried back and forth.

Trains came in, passengers flocked out, everybody in a hurry; while other crowds hurried as fast in the opposite direction, to get aboard trains going out. Bob and Betty were bewildered by the sight of so many people all going their different ways, and each knowing where to go to, for it seemed to them to be only a great confusion.

They had to make room for streams of baggage trucks, great trucks loaded high with the trunks and bags of outgoing passengers; and express packages without number. They watched them all being stowed away into the baggage car. There seemed to be more than the car could hold, but still more were always coming, and room was found for them.

Now, as it grew dark, the lights shone out. Long lines of bright train windows running off in a diminishing perspective, continued outside the station by other lines, other trains either coming or going.

It was all very bewildering, though fascinating, and the children were glad when their father appeared and they were safe on board their own train on their way home.

# THE DINING CAR

This year the children's father had to go on a long journey across the country, on account of his business, and he decided to take the whole family with him. Bob and Betty were delighted; this would indeed be an ideal vacation, to travel so many days in the train, and see so many strange places.

Preparations were made, the house closed, and off they started on the day set. Out from the great depot they sped, stopping at small stations along the way to take on more passengers going in their direction. Sometimes they would stop at large cities for a day or so. And then off on another train and away they would go, crossing state after state.

From the car windows what they saw was all very novel. And the country and the farming along the line was always changing. At times they ran through great wheat belts, where, in every direction, as far as they could see, the wheat was growing. And here the work seemed to be carried on in a wholesale way. The

reaping was done by great machines drawn by sometimes as many as thirty horses. It was all so very different from the way they had seen it at their uncle's farm, where it was cut by men with scythes. Bob and Betty could see all this while taking their meals on the train, for the dining car was just like a restaurant, a fascinating car, where they had their table, and everything served just as comfortably as though they were in town.

Daily, through the trip, they were allowed to go into the baggage car, to see "Sport," their little dog companion, for he too was of the party, though he had to travel in a box. He didn't like it at all, and always welcomed them affectionately. This baggage car was a delight to Bob and Betty. Here were all sorts of things, express packages, from baby carriages to milk cans. And, of course, the passengers' baggage. And Betty and Bob even saw their own trunks. They had always marveled at finding them in the stations wherever they stopped for a day. This wonderful baggage man seemed to know all about everybody's trunk and just where to put it off to meet them. He also became a sort of hero in their eyes, for they couldn't understand how he did it.

# THE SLEEPING CAR

Now I suppose you wonder where Bob and Betty slept when night came on. In their seats? Not at all, for instead they had very comfortable beds. The car they rode in during the daytime was in a way something like those bureaus which let down at night and become beds. But this car "let itself down" into many beds.

When it came time for sleep the porters would skillfully dispose the lower seats into couches, then let down other beds above, folded out of sight in the daytime. Quickly and deftly they would make these up, hang heavy curtains before them, and make a series of little sleeping-rooms, each with two beds, one above the other.

Bob and Betty enjoyed this most ingenious transformation. It was, to them, like something from the "Arabian Nights," and they watched for it every night with fresh enthusiasm. They of course had the upper berths, their parents taking the lower ones.

When the passengers were comfortably stowed away for the night, trying to sleep — Bob and Betty never had to try; they slept without trouble — the porter would darken the car, and all would be quiet.

In the morning the beds were neatly folded up out of the way, and the car became an everyday car again.

Bob and Betty became quite well acquainted with the conductor, and to entertain them, he showed them the sights, such as the baggage car and the mail car, for on this train there was a car which was really a sort of traveling post office. Mail bags were thrown on board, the letters were distributed in different bags, and thrown off at the different stations they should go to, all ready for delivery.

Bob and Betty, of course, had seen many letters come to their house, but they had never known anything about this.

At certain stations where the train didn't stop the mail bags were hung up near the track and, as the train rushed by, a metal arm reached out and gathered them in.

# OVER THE PRAIRIES

It takes a long time to cross this great country, even by fast trains, and by the time Bob and Betty had reached the broad prairies of the West they felt quite at home living in railroad cars.

Away out here were vast stretches which they crossed, white-tipped mountains in the distance. Occasionally they stopped at some small "water tank" station, where, while a stray passenger got on or off, the engine took in water, filling its tender tank again. These stations were often very picturesque in their surroundings, reminding the children of Buffalo Bill's "Wild West" show. In fact it was through this country that Buffalo Bill, when a young man, passed much of his life. Here he hunted the buffalo, which, at that time, roamed the plains in immense herds. Now all that is changed, the buffalo are all gone.

At these little, lonely stations, Bob and Betty saw here and there Indians sell-

ing pottery or beads, and a stray easy-going Mexican, with his big picturesque hat. And the cowboys, real live cowboys. How the children did admire them! The cowboy is passing away, like the buffalo, but the occasional ones who are still left enjoy riding up to the train and doing stunts, in an accidental sort of way. Bob and Betty's admiration of them was all they could wish.

The children were told all about the opening up of this part of the country and how the Indians of that not very distant day often attacked the settlers, or pioneers traveling with their prairie schooners, their big, tent-covered wagons. It took many years of hard work to change all this, so that trains could run across the plains, and bring with them civilization. For the railroad, they were told, was one of the greatest helps in developing civilization, opening up, as it did, new parts of the country, and making it possible for people to come out and live there.

# CROSSING THE MOUNTAINS

By and by they came to the great mountains, so high that nothing grew on their tops, and where sometimes the snow never melted. Around these mountains the train wound, at times along the bottom of some deep canyon whose sides rose a thousand feet above them. The scenery was grandly beautiful, too magnificent for words. It overawed the children, and many of the grown people as well.

Through these gorges the train crawled, at times crossing some rushing mountain stream, or what, at a distance, seemed but a spider web bridge, steadily climbing upward. For as there was no way of getting around these mountains they had to climb over them.

Two engines were attached to the train, and, slowly puffing and tugging, they climbed, zigzagging around and about, always getting higher and higher, till at last Bob and Betty could see shining far below them the tracks over which

they had passed. Once in a while they went through a tunnel cut out of the solid rock, at other times they skirted near high precipices, which made one dizzy to look over. Up here they might see a lone "pocket hunter," with his "burro," a "prospector," still hunting for undiscovered gold mines. Up, up, till at last they reached the very top, and then, slowly and cautiously, coasted down the other slope, the engines, with brakes set, holding back. It was a wonderful experience, never to be forgotten.

At last came the day when they reached the end of their journey. They had crossed the United States. Here, as usual, they found their trunks and "Sport" waiting for them. And now they settled down for a good long rest.

It was out here that they saw that famous Santa Fé engine, the most mighty monster and the most powerful locomotive in the world. It was pointed out to them to show the development from the little "Rocket" of long ago.

Here Bob and Betty spent their vacation, enjoying all the strange sights of this country so different from their own. With "Sport," they passed many happy hours looking out away off over the wide Pacific, storing up new impressions to tell their friends about when they got back home again to the Atlantic side.